New Music Matters

11-14

1

Chris Hiscock and Marian Metcalfe

Heinemann

Heinemann Educational Publishers
Halley Court, Jordan Hill, Oxford OX2 8EJ
a division of Reed Educational & Professional Publishing Ltd

OXFORD MELBOURNE AUCKLAND
JOHANNESBURG BLANTYRE GABORONE
IBADAN PORTSMOUTH (NH) USA CHICAGO

Heinemann is a registered trademark of Reed Educational & Professional Publishing Ltd

First published 1998

02 10 9 8

British Library Cataloguing in Publication Data
A catalogue record for this book is available from the British Library

ISBN 0 435 81090 1

Typeset and designed by Artistix, Thame, Oxon
Music typesetting by Halstan & Co., Amersham, Bucks
Printed and bound in Spain by Edelvives
Cover design by The Point

Acknowledgements

Grateful thanks are extended to the teachers and pupils at the Grove School, Hastings, Hampden Park School, Eastbourne, Seaford Head Community College, Seaford and William Parker School, Hastings for trialling the projects and offering helpful suggestions and advice. Thanks also to Andy Murray and the directors of Music and pupils of Wells Cathedral School and Seaford Head Community College for providing recordings.

The publishers would like to thank the following for permission to reproduce copyright material:
On the road by Patrick Allen © Patrick Allen on p. 49; *Tintinnabulum* from *Adiemus* by Karl Jenkins © Copyright 1995 by Boosey and Hawkes Music Publishers Ltd. for the world excluding Germany, Austria and Switzerland. Reproduced by permission on pp. 53–4; *Changing Partners* by David Clarke © David Clarke/Mouse Records on p. 43; *Pavane pour une infante défunte* by Ravel reproduced by kind permission of Editions Max Eschig, Paris/United Music Publishers Ltd on pp. 22–3; *Concerto for 2 Pianos and Orchestra in D minor* by Poulenc reproduced by kind permission of Editions Salabert, Paris/United Music Publishers Ltd. on p. 21; *Somewhere along the road* by Rick Kemp © Kempire Music Ltd on p. 4; *Cobowo* arr. R. W. Mitchell © R. W. Mitchell on pp. 15–17; *Eleanor Rigby* words and music by John Lennon and Paul McCartney © Copyright 1966 Northern Songs. Used by permission of Music Sales Ltd. All rights reserved. International copyright secured on pp. 37, 40–41; *When I'm sixty-four* words and music by John Lennon and Paul McCartney © Copyright 1967 Northern Songs. Used by permission of Music Sales Ltd.

All rights reserved. International copyright secured on p. 64; *Tango Argentino* by Matyas Seiber © 1933 Schott Musik International GmbH. & Co. KG, Mainz © renewed 1961. This arrangement by permission © 1997 Schott & Co. Ltd on pp. 31–2; *African Kyrie* © Wolverhampton LEA on p. 50.

The publishers would like to thank the following for permission to reproduce photographs:
p. 7 Getty Images; p. 9 Lebrecht Collection; p. 11 Robbie Jack; p. 12 James Davis Travel Photography; p.13 Gareth Boden/Royal Festival Hall; p.14 Rio Helmi; p.18 The Hutchinson Library; p. 20 Getty Images; p. 28 Performing Arts Library; p. 32 Dea Conway; p.33 The Slide File (picture 1), Mary Evans Picture Library (picture 2), Bridgeman Arts Library/Christie's, London (picture 3), Lebrecht Collection (picture 4); p.35 Bate Collection, University of Oxford (pictures a and b), Performing Arts Library (picture c); p. 43 J. Allan Cash Ltd; p. 52 Redferns Music Picture Library (picture a), Still Pictures/Mark Edwards (picture b), Performing Arts Library (picture c), Action Plus (picture d); p. 54 Meg Sullivan; p.55 e.t. Archive (picture 1), Performing Arts Library (picture 2); p. 56 Nonesuch Records; p.59 Lebrecht Collection; p. 61 Getty Images.

The publishers would like to thank Barbie Kilby for the illustration on p. 24.

Contents

On the way

Somewhere along the road

R. Kemp arr. CH and MM

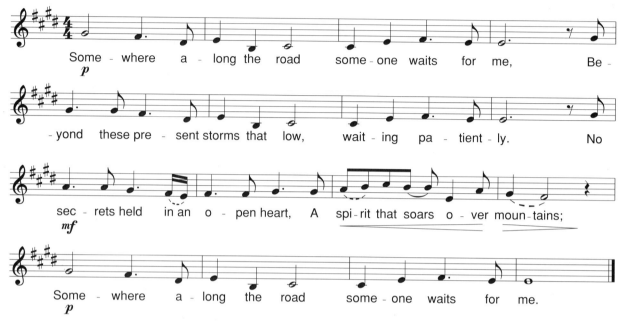

Some - where a - long the road some - one waits for me, Be -
p

- yond these pre - sent storms that low, wait - ing pa - tient - ly. No
mf

sec - rets held in an o - pen heart, A spi - rit that soars o - ver moun - tains;

Some - where a - long the road some - one waits for me.
p

2   Somehow a guiding light always shows the way,
To those who lose their way by night, searching for the day.
A day away from happiness,
Tomorrow will bring a new sunrise;
Somewhere along the road someone waits for me.

3   Sometime when winds are still unexpectedly,
Perhaps beyond this silent hill, a voice will call to me.
Raise your eyes to see my world,
Raise your voice and sing out;
Somewhere along the road someone waits for me.

Counter-melodies to play or sing

Voices or instruments

p Ah_____ (etc.)

mf

p

Changing places

Performing

Choose one of these melodies to play. Notice that:

- each melody has four lines

- in each melody, lines 1, 2 and 4 are the same.

Improvising

Choose one of these ideas for improvising. Use the notes: A C D E G.

Either: Improvise a four-bar melody. Use the same rhythm as the melody you played
Or: Improvise a 16-bar AABA melody. Use the same rhythm as the melody you played
Or: Improvise a 16-bar melody using a rhythm of your own choice.

Sinfonietta

by Leoš Janáček

Fourth movement   track 1

Listen to the fourth movement of this piece by Leoš Janáček. It is made up of one melody repeated many times. You may like to count how many times it repeats the melody.

1a   Which of the following shapes best outlines the melody?

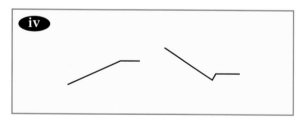

1b   The piece ends with a fast section. *Immediately before* this does the **tempo** speed up or slow down?

Texture   Now listen to track 2

2a   Is the **texture** of the first two repeats thin or thick?
2b   Which instrument plays the tune first?

Timbre and pitch

Now listen to track 3

3a   Which new **timbre** has been added now? Choose one of the following:
   i   brass
   ii   percussion
   iii strings
   iv   woodwind
3b   Are the new notes higher or lower in **pitch** than the melody?

Duration   Now listen to track 4

4   Choose one of the patterns below to describe the **duration** of the backing notes in this excerpt:
   i   short–short–long
   ii   long–long–short
   iii short–long–long

Dynamics   Now listen to track 5

5   Choose one of the following descriptions to match the **dynamics** of the excerpt:
   i   soft–loud–soft–loud
   ii   loud–soft–loud–soft
   iii soft–medium–loud

More about *Sinfonietta*

Sinfonietta is the title of a large piece for a symphony orchestra. It has five separate sections or 'movements'. The fourth movement, which you already know, was originally called *The Street*. Listen to the fourth movement again (track 1). How successful do you think Janáček has been in describing a street?

(Helpful hint: Look at the year in which Janáček was born (see page 9). Think about what a street might have been like when he was old enough to notice. If there weren't many cars in Janáček's time, what else would there have been? And how busy was a city street then?)

Now write a paragraph about Janáček's music, saying whether or not you think it successfully describes a street and why.

First movement

This piece began because Janáček was asked to write some fanfares for brass instruments to be played at a gymnastic display. This gave him the idea for the first movement, and this led to the whole *Sinfonietta*. Listen to the opening of the first movement (track 6) and answer the following questions:

1a The graphics opposite show the shape of three melodies, each of which occurs several times. Write down the order in which you hear each one. All of them are heard several times.

1b Write a sentence about this opening describing:
   i   the timbre
   ii the texture
   iii the dynamics

2 Now listen to the whole of the first movement (track 7) and write a paragraph about how the music is suitable for a gymnastic display.

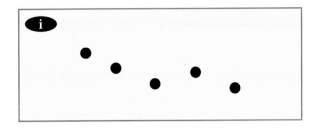

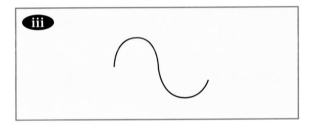

The elements of music

By Key Stage 3 you will already have met the words describing the **elements of music**. These elements are used when discussing and describing music. Because these words are such an important part of your musical vocabulary, you should make sure you know them and can use them correctly when talking or writing about music.

Here is a list of the elements of music. Learn them off by heart.

The Elements of Music	
pitch	is the sound **high** or **low**?
duration	is the sound **long** or **short**?
dynamics	is the volume of the music **loud** or **soft**?
tempo	is the pace of the music **fast** or **slow**?
timbre	what is the **sound of the music** like? e.g. tinny, woody, reedy etc
texture	is the sound of the music **thick** or **thin**? are a lot of instruments playing at once or only a few?

Melody from Symphony From the New World

One of the most satisfying shapes for a melody is ABA or AABA. Discuss with your teacher why this is. Now listen to the opening of the second movement of Dvořák's Symphony *From the New World* (track 8). Some of the melody is based on the notes of the following pentatonic (five note) scale:

Dvořák chose this scale because it was used in many of the spirituals (religious songs sung by slaves in the deep south of America) at that time. He thought that if his melody sounded like a spiritual, he would put some of the feeling of the 'New World' into his music. Follow the melody printed below and then answer the questions.

Note: the music begins with a short introduction before the melody begins.

1 Which of the following shapes best matches the melody?
   i   AABA
   ii   ABC
   iii ABA
   iv   ABAC

2 The B section begins at the beginning of which bar?

3 Choose the correct statements from the following:
a The introduction is played by:
   i   brass
   ii   woodwind
   iii strings
   iv   percussion
b The melody is played by:
   i   a string instrument
   ii   a woodwind instrument
   iii a brass instrument
c The dynamics of the melody are:
   i   loud
   ii   medium
   iii soft
   iv   very soft
d The backing to the melody is played by:
   i   brass
   ii   woodwind
   iii strings
   iv   percussion
e The texture of the excerpt is:
   i   thin
   ii   thick
   iii the texture varies

4 This melody has been used for a TV advert for wholemeal bread. What qualities do you think the music has to make it a good choice to sell wholemeal bread?

5 Write a few lines about American spirituals. Name any others you might have heard or sung yourself. Why do you think they are still so popular?

Two Czechoslovakian composers

Introducing Leoš Janáček

Dates: 1854–1928

Native country: Former Czechoslovakia.

Musical background: Janáček was brought up in a musical family and learned the organ from an early age. He became a choirmaster at the cathedral of Omomou and later, conductor of the Brno Orchestra. His musical development was very slow, and he did not do his best work until he was over forty. In the last twelve years of his life he composed his finest operas and orchestral works.

What types of music did he write best? Opera and music for orchestra.

Why is he remembered? Janáček wrote melodies that sounded like the folk tunes of his own country. He also used folk dance rhythms in his music. He is mainly remembered for his operas and dramatic orchestral music.

Some of his other pieces: *The Makropolous affair* and *Jenufa* (both operas); *Taras Bulba* (orchestral work).

Introducing Anton Dvořák

Dates: 1841–1904

Native country: Former Czechoslovakia.

Musical background: He was the son of an innkeeper and began playing the violin at school. He began an apprenticeship as a butcher before becoming an orchestral player, opera conductor and composer. In 1892 he moved to New York before returning to Prague where he lived for the rest of his life.

What types of music did he write best? Orchestral.

Why is he remembered? He was one of the first composers to take an interest in the folk music of his native country and that of America. He used folk melodies and the scales and rhythms of folk dances in his own music. For this reason he is often labelled a nationalist composer. Dvořák was also very sensitive to the timbres of the orchestra and has since been admired for the mixtures and blend of instruments in his music.

Some of his other pieces: *Slavonic dances*, nine symphonies, *String serenade*.

Melody match

Listen to six melodies (tracks 9–14) and answer the following questions. Write your answers on the pupil sheet, or in your books.

1 Match *the beginning* of each of the following melodies with *one* of the graphic shapes drawn in the boxes below.

a	*Personent hodie* (trad.)	**d**	*Ode to joy* by Beethoven
b	*I've got rhythm* by George Gershwin	**e**	*Take five* by Dave Brubeck
c	*Grande valse brillante* by Chopin	**f**	*Intermezzo* from *Cavalleria rusticana* by Mascagni

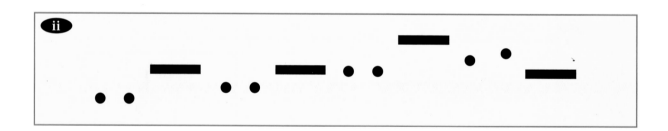

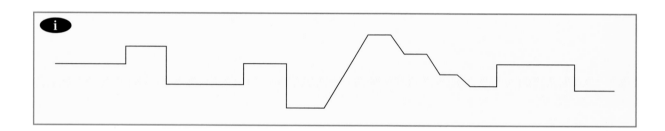

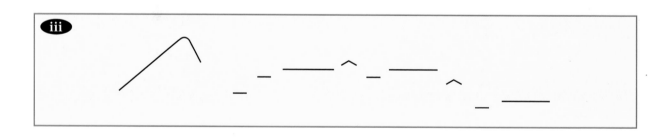

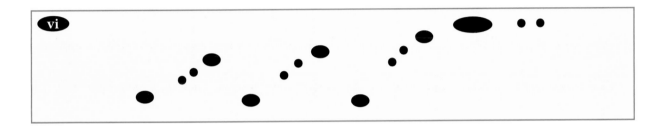

Now listen to all six melodies again.

2   Which of the six melodies has an AABA shape? Write 'yes' or 'no' for each melody.

3   Which melody do you think is the most satisfying to listen to? Write down up to three musical reasons for your choice.

A scene from a production of *Cavalleria rusticana*

The music of Java and Bali

Gamelan is the traditional music from the islands of Indonesia. The word 'gamelan' refers to an ensemble or group of different pitched percussion instruments, mainly metallophones and gongs, with the occasional xylophone or flute. Gamelans sound very metallic when they are played, a little like classroom instruments such as glockenspiels, metallophones and xylophones.

One of the first westerners to hear the gamelan was the English explorer Sir Francis Drake (c1540–96). He described the music: 'which though it were of a very strange kind, yet the sound was pleasant and delightful.'

The islands of Java and Bali both have long traditions of gamelan. Music and dancing are very important in their everyday life and culture. Gamelans are always played by a group of players, never by just one person. Each village has its own gamelan which sounds slightly different from that of every other village.

You can hear gamelan music on all important occasions, at dances, shadow-puppet plays (called 'Wayang Kulit') and as background music in many restaurants, hotels and other public places. Sometimes the gamelan sounds very gentle and delicate, dreamy and shimmering; sometimes it sounds harsh, wild, loud and frantic. Experts often give virtuoso performances, usually at breakneck speed, but they always listen carefully to keep with the ensemble, and play musically to enhance the music of the other players.

Listening to the sound of the gamelan

Listen to three short excerpts of gamelan (tracks 25, 27 and 28) and discuss the differences between each of them with your teacher or your group. The excerpts are:

a   Javanese gamelan
b   Balinese gamelan
c   rindik gamelan

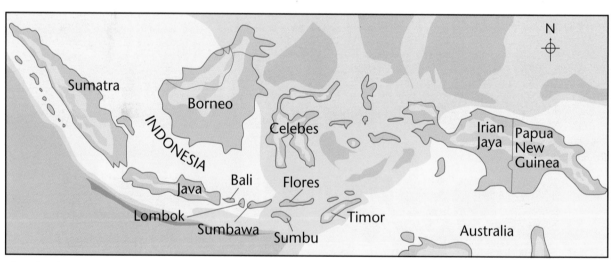

The islands of Indonesia

The instruments of the Javanese gamelan

kempul and gongs

kethuk and kenong

saron and saron penerus

The Javanese gamelan at the
Royal Festival Hall, London

kendhang

bonang

Lancaran Cobowo

arr. R. Mitchell

Gamelan music is built up in layers. At its centre is a basic melody (core melody) known as the **balungan**. The notes of each layer of music relate closely to the balungan and help with decorating it, or with supporting the structure.

The instruments of the gamelan are tuned to:

either   a five-note scale called **slendro**
or   a seven-note scale called **pelog**.

Each note in gamelan music is called by a number. When gamelan players learn a new piece of music they sing the note-numbers of the new melody before playing the notes on instruments, and also while they are practising the piece.

Here are approximately what the notes of the **slendro scale** would be if written in staff notation and with their Javanese note-numbers underneath:

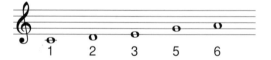

Listening to Lancaran *Cobowo*

Lancaran (pronounced lancharan) is a common form in Javanese composition. Lancaran *Cobowo* (pronounced cho-bo-woh) is 'in' slendro (see opposite).

Listen as Lancaran *Cobowo* is gradually built up into a performance. Notice the way it is built up in layers. Follow the printed music on the pages 15–17 whilst you listen to each excerpt.

To perform Lancaran *Cobowo*

1   Listen to the way in which Lancaran *Cobowo* is built up in the demonstration performance.

2   Learn to play each part in turn, and gradually put them together into a class gamelan piece.

3   Check that you have each part right by listening to the demonstration excerpt again until you are satisfied.

Note: the best instruments to use for your performance are glockenspiels and xylophones. However, other instruments may be used. Keyboards, for example, should use voices that sound similar to pitched percussion.

A Balinese gamelan uses similar instruments to a Javanese one

Layer 1 (track 15)

Sarons
The balungan (core melody) is played on the sarons. The Javanese note-numbers are printed as well as the western letter-names. Sing the note-numbers as you play the notes.

D E D G   E D E G   A C A G   E A G E
2 3 2 5   3 2 3 5   6 1 6 5   3 6 5 3

Peking
The peking plays the balungan at a higher pitch in pairs of repeated notes.

D E D G   E D E G   A C A G   E A G E
2 3 2 5   3 2 3 5   6 1 6 5   3 6 5 3

Kethuk
The kethuk is often referred to as the 'time-keeper'. It plays in between the beats and is very important as it keeps the pulse steady.

Layer 2 (track 16)

Kenong
The next layer is played by the kenong (the 'sitting gong'). The notes of the kenong part are based on important notes of the balungan.

D   E   E   A   A   E   E   D
2   3   3   6   6   3   3   2

Layer 3 (track 17)

Kempul and gongs (gong suwukan, gong ageng)
The kempul and gongs play the most important notes of the balungan. They sound at important places to mark the structure, and to tell the players where they are in the balungan.

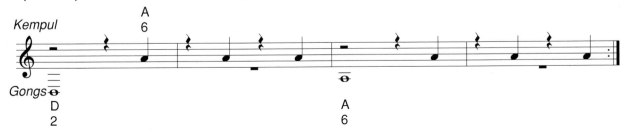

Layer 4 (track 18)

Bonang barung (with saron, peking, kethuk, kenong and gongs)

The bonang barung plays notes based on the core melody. It fits them *in between* the notes of the core melody.

Layer 5 (track 19)

Bonang penerus (added to the texture so far)

The bonang penerus plays a rhythmic variation based on the same notes as the bonang barung.

Layer 6 (track 20)

Kendhang added

Hand drums or kendhang are used to control the performance. They give aural cues to the performers, telling them when to begin, when to end, and when to change from one section to the next.

There are two drums used in this piece, the **kendhang ageng** (larger drum), and the **kendhang ketipung** (smaller drum). The syllables describe the sound of each drum stroke according to where the drum head is struck:

dung – strike the right-hand side of the kendhang ketipung, allowing the drum to resonate.
dah – strike the right-hand side of the larger kendhang ageng.

A simple drum pattern is repeated throughout the balungan. It combines with it as follows:

Layer 7 (track 21)

Counter-melody (played by a few sarons)

A new tune is added on a few of the sarons. Be careful that the counter-melody does not drown the balungan.

Layer 8 (track 22)

Buka (introduction)

A simple introduction called a **buka** begins Lancaran *Cobowo*. It is played on the bonang barung. Follow the Javanese notation as you listen. (The western letter-names are included in brackets.)

First note of balungan

| Bonang Buka | 6 | 6 | • | 6 | 5 | 6 | 3 | • | 6 | • | 5 | 2 2 | • | 2 2 | ②(Gong) |

| Western notation | (A | A | • | A | G | A | E | • | A | • | G | D D | • | D D | •) |

Kendhang introduction begins here

Now compare the western staff notation on pages 15 and 16 with the Javanese notation printed below.

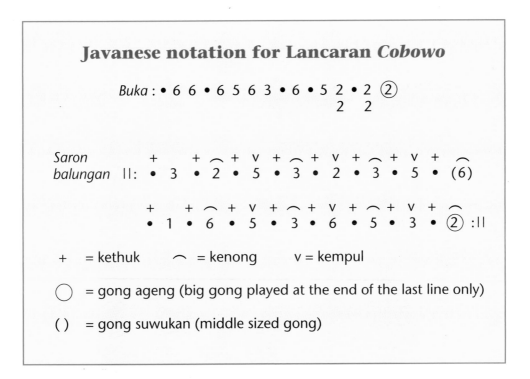

Javanese notation for Lancaran *Cobowo*

Buka : • 6 6 • 6 5 6 3 • 6 • 5 2 • 2 ②
2   2

Saron balungan ‖:
+ • 3 + • 2⌒ + • 5v + • 3⌒ + • 2v + • 3⌒ + • 5v + • (6)⌒

+ • 1 + • 6⌒ + • 5v + • 3⌒ + • 6v + • 5⌒ + • 3v + • ②⌒ :‖

+ = kethuk   ⌒ = kenong   v = kempul

◯ = gong ageng (big gong played at the end of the last line only)

( ) = gong suwukan (middle sized gong)

Points to notice:

- Javanese notation looks much simpler when compared with staff notation. This is because there is much less detail included.
- The bonang and kendhang parts are not included. The bonang and kendhang players are expected to work out their own parts from the balungan according to traditional practice.

Gamelan music from Bali: rindik

The Lancaran music of Java was traditionally court music. It was played for important people, and a number of people were needed to perform it.

However, in the smaller villages of Bali, a style of gamelan called **rindik** is more common. The music that it produces is very gentle, and is considered the true folk music of Bali. Rindik music is heard in everyday settings, in homes, hotels and restaurants.

This type of gamelan music consists of two bamboo xylophones and a flute (compare photo below with photo on p14).

Listening to rindik *Tabuh telu*
(track 28)

This typical rindik piece has three layers:

a   A core melody which is played as repeated single-beat notes on the lower end of each bamboo xylophone. This means that the core melody is played with the left hand by *both* xylophone players.

b   The same core melody played smoothly on the flute.

c   An interlocking melody called **kotekan**. In kotekan a single melody is divided between the two xylophone players. They play in half beat notes at the high end of each xylophone. This means that kotekan is played with the right hand by *both* xylophone players.

Rindik performance in a Balinese village

Performing Tempung ketan

As a whole class or in groups of four or five, perform *Tempung ketan* below.

If you are working in groups, choose one or two people to play core melody 1. Remember to select people who can keep a steady beat.

Next choose one or two people to play core melody 2. They need to be able to feel the pulse right through the long notes so they always come in at the right place. Core melody 2 will sound best on a flute or recorder. If you do not have anyone in your group who can play either of these, choose an instrument which can sustain its notes.

The kotekan part is optional. If you decide to attempt it, it should be performed by two members of your group. The two parts are called **lanang** (boy) and **wadon** (girl). The kotekan part should begin halfway through the core melody as shown below, and continue throughout the piece.

Note that there is *no* buka (introduction), so you will have to decide how to begin your piece. Notice, too, that there are no drums in this piece.

Tempung ketan

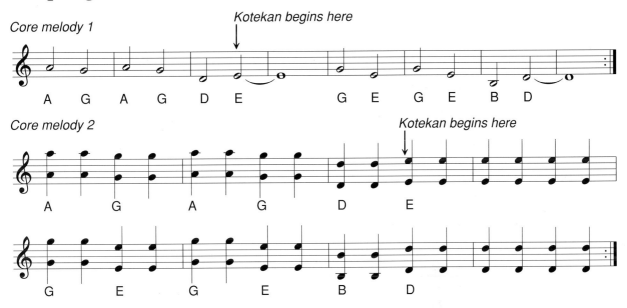

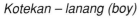

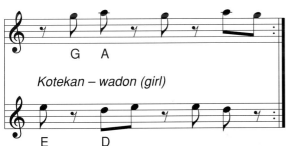

Westward from Java and Bali

Western music inspired by gamelan

In 1889, the city of Paris held a Grand Universal Exhibition to mark the centenary of the French Revolution. The exhibition was made famous because of one exhibit, a gigantic structure built by Monsieur Eiffel.

The Eiffel Tower, as it became known, along with many other strange exhibits, drew crowds from Europe and beyond. For the first time ordinary Europeans were brought face to face with the buildings, costumes, customs, dances, music and theatre of other continents. The exhibition made a great impression on all those who attended.

One of the visiting groups from Asia was a gamelan from Java. The strange and mysterious sounds of the gamelan inspired new compositions from a whole generation of French composers who were thrilled by its music. Following the Paris Exhibition, the gamelan continued to inspire many composers and musicians in the twentieth century.

Listening to gamelan-inspired music

Listen to two different excerpts of music written by western composers who were inspired by the gamelan.

As you listen, answer the questions opposite in your book.

The Indo-Chinese pavilion at the Paris exhibition

A *Concerto for two pianos* by Francis Poulenc   **(track 29)**

1   This music has a number of sections. Choose *one* of the following lists to match the order of the sections.

A	B	C
pianos	pianos	pianos
pianos and orchestra	pianos and xylophone	pianos and orchestra
pianos	orchestra	orchestra
pianos and solo string instrument	brass and piccolo	pianos and solo brass instrument
pianos and orchestra	pianos	orchestra

2   Which of the following words describe the feeling and mood of this music? You may choose more than one word if you like. Or you may choose a word of your own.

    violent   dreamy   joyful   floating   mysterious

                  shimmering   energetic

3   Which instruments *that you can hear in the music* are used to copy the sound of a gamelan?

4   How many times is the following melody heard in the excerpt?

B *Princess of the Pagodas* from *Mother Goose suite* by Maurice Ravel   **(track 30)**

1   Complete a copy of the chart below by placing these sections in the order in which they are heard. Two have been done for you.

introduction   glockenspiels and brass answered by flutes

unison melody with gongs   solo flute and piccolo melodies

mainly xylophones and flutes   repeating solo woodwind melodies with some xylophone notes

i	introduction	iv	
ii		v	
iii	glockenspiels and brass answered by flutes	vi	

2   Which section sounds most like the gamelan? Why?

Pavane pour une infante défunte

by Ravel arr. CH

Alto glock

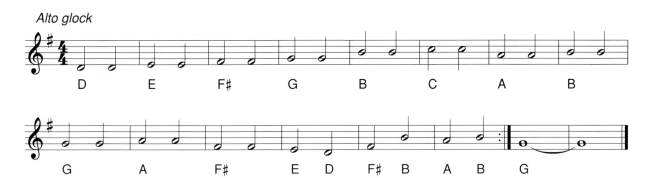

Metallophone

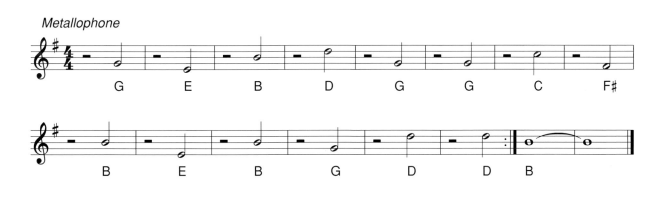

Bass metallophone

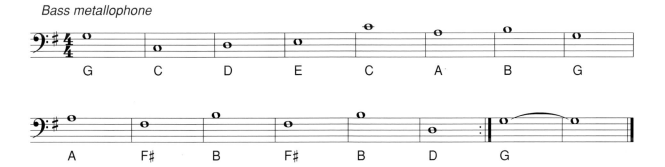

Major and minor

Joshua fought the Battle of Jericho

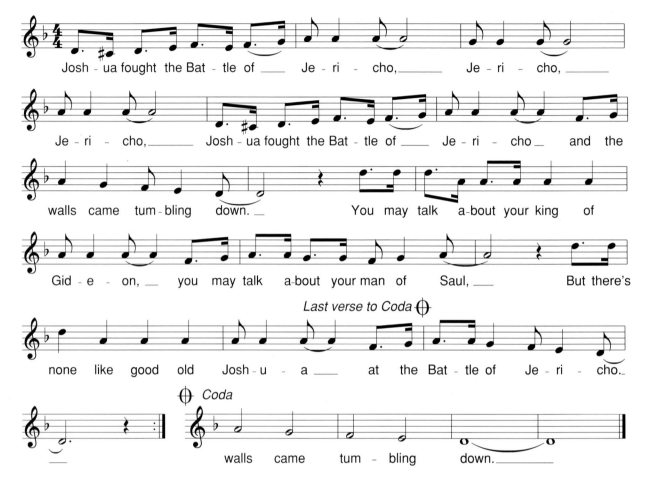

Josh – ua fought the Bat – tle of ___ Je – ri – cho, ___ Je – ri – cho, ___

Je – ri – cho, ___ Josh – ua fought the Bat – tle of ___ Je – ri – cho ___ and the

walls came tum – bling down. __ You may talk a-bout your king of

Gid – e – on, __ you may talk a-bout your man of Saul, ___ But there's

Last verse to Coda ⊕

none like good old Josh – u – a ___ at the Bat – tle of Je – ri – cho. _

⊕ *Coda*

___ walls came tum – bling down.

2   Joshua fought the Battle of Jericho,
       Jericho, Jericho,
    Joshua fought the Battle of Jericho
       and the walls came tumbling down.
    Up to the walls of Jericho,
       he marched with spear in hand,
    'Go sound those ram horns,' Joshua cried,
       'cos the battle is in my hand.'

3   Joshua fought the Battle of Jericho,
       Jericho, Jericho,
    Joshua fought the Battle of Jericho
       and the walls came tumbling down.
    Then the lam-ram sheep horns began to play,
       and the trumpets they did sound,
    Joshua commanded all the people to shout,
       and the walls came tumbling down.

'Go sound those ram horns,' Joshua cried

Counter-melody (scale of D minor)

Counter-melody (Scale of D minor)

Improvisation section

DC

Last verse

* This curved line is a **tie**. Hold the second note on instead of playing it again.

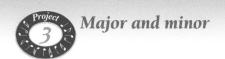

Major and minor

Bass melody (scale of D minor)

Bass melody (Scale of D minor)

Improvisation section

Last verse

* This curved line is a **tie**. Hold the second note on instead of playing it again.

Major and minor scales

Most music is composed using a particular pattern of notes called a **scale.** There are many different scales, each with its own special pattern. Two very popular ones are the **major scale** and the **minor scale.** Each scale has its own pattern made up of **tones** and **semitones.**

A semitone is the name given to the distance between two next-door notes on a piano or keyboard. Next-door notes can be black or white. A semitone measures the difference in pitch between these notes.

A tone equals two next-door semitones. It measures the difference in pitch between two notes on a piano or keyboard which have only one note in between them.

Major scales

Major scales have the following pattern of tones and semitones:

Tone   Tone   Semitone   Tone   Tone   Tone   Semitone

e.g. when the first note of a major scale is D, the rest of the scale is:

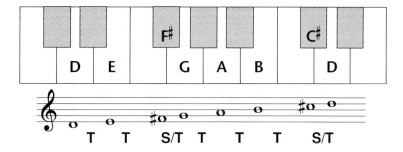

Minor scales

There are two types of minor scale. One type is the **harmonic minor scale.** It has the following pattern of tones and semitones:

Tone   Semitone   Tone   Tone   Semitone   Tone *plus* Semitone   Semitone

e.g. when the first note of a harmonic minor scale is D, the rest of the scale is:

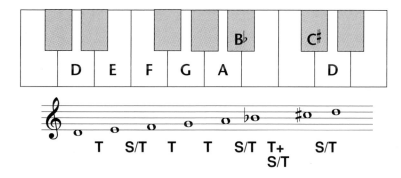

Practise the major and minor scales on D until you can play them easily.

Now practise working out other scales using the patterns of tones and semitones to help you. Try beginning on G, E and A. Have fun!

That's love (Habanera)

Listening to *That's love* (track 31)

First listen to *That's love* and test yourself on major and minor.

1 Is the beginning of *That's love* in:
   i a major key?
   ii a minor key?

2 On which word or words does the music change mode (i.e. from major to minor *or* from minor to major)?

3 What difference does this change of mode have on the *mood* of the song?

The story of *Carmen*

That's love comes from an opera called *Carmen*. An opera is a play set to music where the words are sung rather than spoken. *Carmen* is a very famous opera by a French composer named Georges Bizet (1838–75). It is based on a story by the French writer Prosper Merimée.

Carmen is a Spanish gypsy girl who is working in a factory when the story opens. She sees the soldier Don José one lunchtime and decides to make him fall in love with her even though he already has a girlfriend. At first he isn't interested, but Carmen has a way with her and soon she captures his heart.

Don José deserts the army and leaves his girlfriend Micaela to be with Carmen, but Carmen soon gets tired of him and instead takes up with Escamillo, the hunky bullfighter who she thinks is much more glamorous than Don José. José is desperately unhappy at this and tries very hard to persuade Carmen to come back to him. She refuses and instead goes to watch Escamillo in a major bullfight.

José waits for Carmen outside the ring and gives her one last chance to come back to him, but she only laughs at him. Then José says that if he can't have her, no one will. He takes out a knife and stabs her. Carmen dies as José is arrested and led away, while inside the ring the crowd cheers as Escamillo wins the bullfight.

That's love is sung by Carmen when she first appears on stage. The words tell the audience about her character, that she is fickle and faithless and just out for what she can get.

Carmen is one of the most popular and famous operas in the world. It is performed many times each year. If you are able to listen to it, you will probably find that you already know several of the tunes because they are played so often.

A scene from a production of *Carmen*

That's love (Habanera)

from *Carmen* by Bizet, trans. Klein

Score-reading

Practise following the music as you listen to the song. The numbers in boxes at the beginning of each line are bar numbers so that you can find the number of any bar quickly when you want to talk about it.

First learn 1 and 2 what they mean.

Next, with your teacher, make sure you know that the music goes from bar 1–47, and then from bar 4–48.

Now clap the rhythm of the **habanera** several times to become familiar with it. The habanera is a Spanish dance. (Remember *Carmen* is set in Spain.)

Next move your finger along the lines in time with the beat. You may need to slow down or pause here and there. Keep listening and 'go with the flow'.

If you have it right you should end up in bar 48 as the music stops.

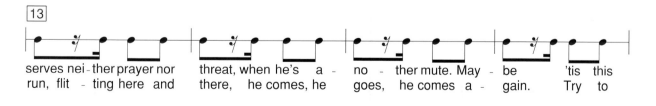

Tango Argentino

M. Seiber adapted CH

Part 3   *D minor*

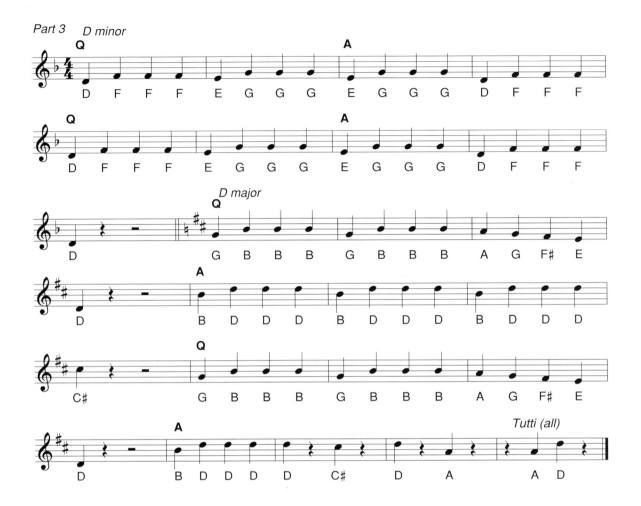

Dancing the tango

Listening to contrasts in dance music

Dancing is as old as humankind. It is part of the life of every culture and every people. Dancing has always been a part of much ceremony and ritual. And wherever there is a celebration, festivity, or entertainment, there is nearly always dancing.

Listen to four pieces of dance-like music (tracks 32–35). Each one has a picture showing how the dance might have looked.

Below are four boxes of statements. Listen carefully to each piece of music and find one statement from each box which matches each dance.

Write the name of each dance as a heading, and write the statements you have chosen underneath.

1 *The Cherry Blossom* – trad

Traditional Irish dancing

a
i	major key
ii	minor key

b
i	flute, strings & harpsichord
ii	full orchestra
iii	medieval instruments
iv	traditional folk instruments – uilleann pipes, harp & guitar

c
i	two beats in a bar
ii	three beats in a bar

3 *Ungaresca* by Mainiero

Peasants dancing at a village wedding

d
i	this piece is based on a well-known tune played in a Spanish dance rhythm
ii	this piece has two sections and repeats each of them
iii	the melody of this piece is played three times
iv	this piece has a drone throughout

2 *Badinerie* by J. S. Bach

Courtly dancing in the eighteenth century

4 Variation on *America* by Ives/Schuman

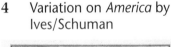

Dancing the bolero

Working with chords

Music for special occasions

The opera *Orfeo* was composed by the Italian Monteverdi in 1607. It was commissioned by the Duke of Mantua, and was one of the very first operas to be composed. It was performed as part of the carnival celebrations leading up to Lent (the season before Easter).

Monteverdi begins his opera with a short **overture** (introduction) like a **fanfare**. This announces the mood of the occasion, and would certainly have attracted the attention of all who listened.

Follow the printed melody of the piece above as you listen to track 36. It is played on violins and cornetts. A cornett (spelt with two 't's) is an ancient ebony instrument that is a cross between a recorder and a trumpet.

One of the most striking things to notice in this overture is Monteverdi's use of backing melodies which sound like fanfares. The main melody is backed up with several fanfare melodies played at the same time.

Fanfares are short pieces of music composed to attract attention, e.g. the arrival of an important person, the beginning of a special occasion, or the opening of a play. Before the invention of modern communications equipment, fanfares were used to send signals to troops on a noisy battlefield. Fanfares were most often played by trumpets, bugles and drums because they could play loudly and the tone carried well.

In earlier times, trumpets, like bugles, had no valves (these were invented in the late eighteenth century) and could only play melodies using the following notes.

These notes are called the **harmonic series**.

When the first five notes of the harmonic series are sounded together, we hear the chord of C. Play the first five notes of the harmonic series together and listen to the sound of the chord of C:

Chord of C

C, G, C, E, G: you can add top C if you like

Introducing chords

When two or more notes are played together, the sound that you hear is called a **chord**. The commonest type of chord is a three note chord or **triad**.

To play the triad of C, find **C** first and then miss out D, play **E**, miss out F, play **G**. Play all three notes together to make the triad of C. These three notes come from the harmonic series.

The sound of all three notes played together in this way is also described as a **block chord**.

Remember, to make a triad, play one note, miss one, play one, miss one, play one.

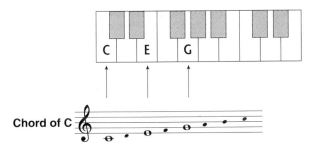

Chord of C

Chords are most often used as an accompaniment to melodies. They make the texture of music thicker and give melodies a fuller sound.

The three notes of a chord may also be split up and arranged into patterns. Then they are often called **broken chords**. Chord melodies or broken chords can create attractive backings. They are frequently used instead of block chords because they are more flowing.

Work out and play each of the following chords: **C**, **G** and **F**. You will learn more about these three chords later in the project.

A   Cornett

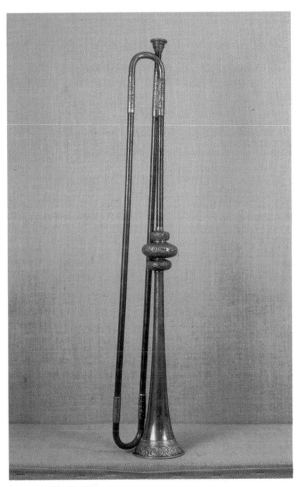

B   Valveless trumpet

C   Modern trumpet

Listening to Monteverdi's Vespers

Latin words	English translation
1 Deus in adiutorium meum intende,	O God, make haste to save me,
2 Domine ad adiuvandum me festina,	O Lord, make haste to help me,
3 Gloria Patri et Filio	Glory be to the Father, and to the Son,
4 et Spiritui Sancto:	and to the Holy Spirit:
5 Sicut erat in principio et nunc et semper,	As it was in the beginning, is now, and ever shall be,
6 et in saecula saeculorum.	world without end.
7 Amen. Alleluia.	Amen. Alleluia.

Listen to a second piece by Monteverdi (track 37). This is the opening of *Vespers*, which is a religious piece for choir, solo voices and instruments. *Vespers* uses the same musical material as the overture from *Orfeo*. However, in this piece, the choir sings the notes of a single chord together, whilst fanfares and other melodies make up a very grand accompaniment.

In this excerpt, Monteverdi composes most of the music by using just one single chord.

Follow the Latin words printed above, and answer the questions underneath. The lines of words are numbered to help you.

1 Choose a word or words from the following to describe how line 1 is sung:
   i   unison
   ii   solo
   iii descant
   iv   accompanied
   v   unaccompanied

2 The instruments change chord in *three* different places in the music. Pinpoint these three places as accurately as you can. (Use the line numbers and words to help you.)

3 The choir only change the chord they are singing on *one* word.
   a   on which word does this happen?
   b   what else is different about the setting of this word?

4 Which families of instruments are used in this piece?

5 Write one or more sentences saying why you think this music is suitable for a special occasion. What particular features in the music make you think this?

More things to do

6 Find out and write about each of the following instruments heard in Monteverdi's orchestra. Include a picture if you can.
   a   sackbuts
   b   cornetts
   c   viols
   d   harpsichord
   e   lute

7 Find out about:
   a   The Medici family in Florence who commissioned the very first opera, *Euridice* by the composer Peri.
   b   The story of *Orpheus and Euridice*, upon which Monteverdi's *Orfeo* is based. (*Orpheus and Euridice* is a famous ancient Greek legend.)
   c   St Mark's Cathedral in Venice, where Monteverdi's *Vespers* were performed.

Eleanor Rigby

John Lennon and Paul McCartney arr. CH

Ah ___ look at all ___ the lone - ly peo - ple. ___

1 E - lea-nor Rig - by ___ picks up the rice ___ in the church ___ where a wed - ding has been,

___ Lives in a dream. ___ Waits at the win - dow, ___

wear-ing the face ___ that she keeps ___ in a jar ___ by the door, ___

Who is it for? ___ All the lone - ly peo - ple, where do ___ they all come

from? All the lone - ly peo - ple, where do ___ they all ___ be - long? ___

Em   **C**

2   Father McKenzie, writing the words of a service that no one will hear,
No one comes near.
Em   **C**
Look at him working, darning his socks in the night when there's nobody there,
What does he care?
Em7   **Em6**   **C/E**   **Em**
All the lonely people, where do they all come from?
Em7   **Em6**   **C/E**   **Em**
All the lonely people, where do they all belong?

Em   **C**

3   Eleanor Rigby died in a church and was buried along with her name,
Nobody came.
Em   **C**
Father McKenzie, wiping the dirt from his hands as he walks from the grave,
No one was saved.
Em7   **Em6**   **C/E**   **Em**
All the lonely people, where do they all come from?
Em7   **Em6**   **C/E**   **Em**
All the lonely people, where do they all belong?

Backing Eleanor Rigby using two chords

The backing to *Eleanor Rigby* by John Lennon and Paul McCartney is based mainly on two chords. These are E minor (**Em**) and **C**.

Like major and minor scales, chords are also described as major or minor. (You will learn more about the difference between major and minor chords later.)

Look at these two chords on the keyboard diagrams:

Chord of E minor

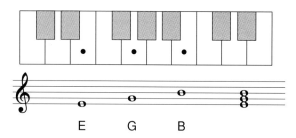

E   G   B

Chord of C

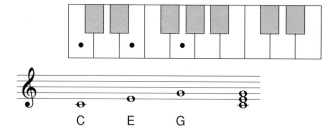

C   E   G

Playing a chord in time to the beat

When we want to strum or play the same chord in time with the beat, it is often written like this:

4 beats in a bar

	Em	/	/	/	C	/	/	/
count	1	2	3	4	1	2	3	4

Now practise moving from Em to C like this until you can do it easily:

play
Em / / / **C** / / / **Em** / / / **C** / / /
count   etc.
  1 2 3 4 1 2 3 4   1 2 3 4 1 2 3 4

Chord symbols are often added to the music above the melody of a song. The chords are then played in a way that fits the style of the song.

Look at the way that Em and C are written above the melody to *Eleanor Rigby* on page 37.

Note: The chords of Em7 and Em6 are indicated. Both chords have four notes, i.e. Em7 has E, G, B, D and Em6 has E, G, B, C#. If you can't manage to play all four notes, leave out the top note of each and simply play the chord of Em instead.

Before you play the chords to accompany *Eleanor Rigby*, practise the chord sequence on its own until you can play it successfully.

count																				
1	2	3	4	1	2	3	4	1	2	3	4	1	2	3	4	1	2	3	4
verse																			
Em	/	/	/	Em	/	/	/	Em	/	/	/	C	/	/	/	C	/	/	/
Em	/	/	/	Em	/	/	/	Em	/	/	/	C	/	/	/	C	/	/	/
chorus																			
Em7	/	/	/	Em6	/	/	/	C/E	/	/	/	Em	/	/	/				
Em7	/	/	/	Em6	/	/	/	C/E	/	/	/	Em	/	/	/				

Chords into riffs

What is a riff?

Riff is a word used in rock music. It describes a short pattern made from the notes of a chord.

Sometimes a riff also adds the notes that lie in between the chord notes (see riff 3 below). These notes are called **passing notes**.

When the chord changes, the riff pattern remains the same but the notes change to the notes of the new chord.

Adding riffs to *Eleanor Rigby*

Below are three riffs that can be used as extra backing parts to *Eleanor Rigby*. Play each riff, and practise changing from the Em chord to the C chord as shown.

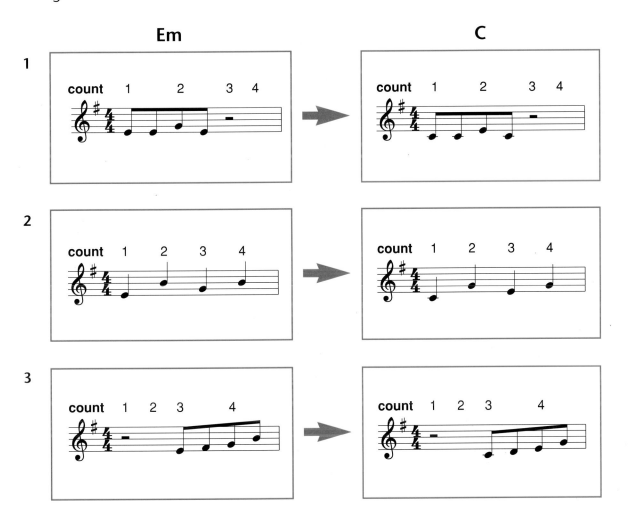

On pages 40–41 you will find some backing parts for *Eleanor Rigby*. These are built on the three riffs you have just learnt.

Either: Perform the backing parts to *Eleanor Rigby* on pages 40–41.

Or: Use the riffs above, and arrange your own backing from them. Use the chord symbols on the music of *Eleanor Rigby* on page 37 to tell you when to change chords

Or: Compose your own riffs, and arrange your own backing from them. Use the chord symbols on the music of *Eleanor Rigby* on page 37 to tell you when to change chords.

39

Eleanor Rigby in parts

John Lennon and Paul McCartney arr. CH

Learning more about chords

Chords can be built on all seven notes of any major or minor scale. These seven chords then provide a **chord bank** to choose from when backing a melody. To choose from the correct chord bank you need to know the scale, or **key**, in which the melody has been composed.

Below are the seven chords built on the notes of the C major scale.

Triads in the key of C major

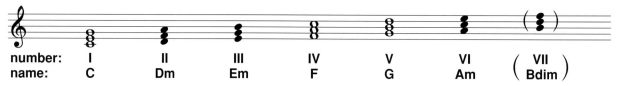

number:	I	II	III	IV	V	VI	(VII	)
name:	C	Dm	Em	F	G	Am	Bdim	

Notice that each of these seven chords is named in two different ways:

a   by its **root** note (the note of the scale upon which the chord is built) and its type, i.e. whether or not it is:

   major: a chord in which the interval between the root and the middle note of the triad is four semitones (called a **major third**)

   or **minor:**   a chord in which the interval between the root and the middle note of the triad is three semitones (called a **minor third**)

b   by a Roman numeral according to which note of the scale it is built on.

Primary chords

In any major or minor scale, three chords are used more often than the others. These are chords I, IV and V. They are known as the **primary chords**.

In the scale of C major shown above, the primary chords are C (I), F (IV) and G (V). These three chords between them contain every note of the major scale. This means that every note of a melody composed in a major scale can be **harmonized** by at least one of the three primary chords.

Play the three primary chords in the key of C major (C, F, G). Now practise changing between them, using the chord changes, known as **chord progressions**, below. Practise these until they are fluent as you will need them later on.

1	count	1	2	3	4	1	2	3	4	1	2	3	4	1	2	3	4
	chord	C	/	/	/	C	/	/	/	F	/	/	/	F	/	/	/
2	count	1	2	3	4	1	2	3	4	1	2	3	4	1	2	3	4
	chord	C	/	/	/	C	/	/	/	G	/	/	/	G	/	/	/
3	count	1	2	3	4	1	2	3	4	1	2	3	4	1	2	3	4
	chord	C	/	/	/	F	/	C	/	C	/	/	/	G	/	C	/

Steel pans music from the Caribbean

Steel bands began in Trinidad when a great many oil drums were left lying around after World War II. It was soon found that they could be turned into musical instruments.

Steel pans are made by cutting oil drums into different sizes and then beating the tops into concave bowls. Each individual note is then beaten into a small area of the bowl. Small rubber-headed sticks are used to strike each note.

These days a steel band consists of a number of different-sized steel pans, and a rhythm section of Latin-American percussion instruments. Each pan or pair of pans has its own name according to its pitch-range. Some of the pans have more than one name although they mean the same thing.

A steel band performing in a street carnival in Antigua

names of the pans	the part they play in the band
soprano, ping pong, or first tenor	usually play the melody
double alto, double second, or second tenor	play a second melody underneath the soprano part
single alto	play two-note chords
cello, or guitar	play chords, tune, or bass
bass	play the bass part

The picture opposite shows the note positions on a soprano pan.

Because a wide range of pitches is available on steel pans, the steel band is a very versatile ensemble. Many different styles of music can be performed, including traditional Caribbean, pop and classical music. However, the steel band is most often found in outdoor carnivals playing traditional Caribbean music.

Listen to *Changing partners* (track 38) performed by The Ebony Steel Band who came from the islands of Trinidad and Grenada. Notice the following features of music for steel pans:

- The way the notes of the tune are lengthened by 'rolling' the sticks like a drum roll. This prevents long notes dying away too rapidly.

- In the same way, the backing chords are 'lengthened' by using a riff on the first two beats of each bar.

- The rhythm is kept steady by the bass notes, and off-beat chords played on the cello pans.

Now try this: the chord pattern of *Changing partners* is printed below with some gaps. Decide what is missing using chords I, IV, and V. There are four beats in each bar.

I / / /	I / / /	I / / /	IV / / /	II / / /	V / / /	? / / /	? / / /
I / / /	I / / /	I / / /	? / / /	II / / /	I / / /	IV / ? /	? / / /

Performing Charley Marley

Charley Marley is an arrangement of a traditional Caribbean song for steel band. If your school has a set of steel pans, use these for this song. If not, perform the parts on appropriately pitched instruments, sharing out the chord notes where necessary. Use pre-set steel pans voices on keyboards if these are available.

The piece is based on the three primary chords of C major: C, F and G. Practise the chord sequences below before performing the arrangement. Practise the repeats too.

Charley Marley chord sequence (cello and bass pans)

Section A
count   1 2 3 4 1 2 3 4 1 2 3 4 1 2 3 4
chord ‖: C / / / C / / / G / / / C / / / :‖

                                     ↑
                          (repeat sign)

Section B
count   1 2 3 4 1 2 3 4 1 2 3 4 1 2 3 4
chord ‖: C / / / C / / / G / / / C / / / :‖

Section C
count   1 2 3 4 1 2 3 4 1 2 3 4 1 2 3 4
chord ‖: F / / / C / / / G / / / C / / / :‖

Notice that in *Charley Marley*, the chord notes are split between the cello and bass pans in the rhythm 'oom cha-cha oom cha'.

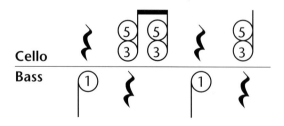

Charley Marley melody (soprano and alto pans)

The melody of *Charley Marley* is arranged for the soprano and alto pans. It has three sections: A, B and C. Practise all three sections before performing the whole piece together.

> You may also like to sing the words of the song as you play (sing the notes an octave lower when you need to):
>
> **Section A**
> Right through, right through the rocky road, Sing Charley Marley call you. *(twice)*
>
> **Section B**
> Any girl I don' like I don' call to them, Sing Charley Marley call you, Any boy I don' like I don' call to them, Sing Charley Marley call you.
>
> **Section C**
> Right through, right through the rocky road, Sing Charley Marley call you. *(twice)*

Charley Marley performance plan

Charley Marley is a traditional children's game which usually continues until all the children have had a turn. The following order is suggested for performance:

A   A   B   B   A   A   C   C   A   A

However, at a carnival or other festivity, the piece might be shortened or lengthened to fit the time available. Decide on the right order of the sections for your class performance.

Charley Marley

Jamaican folk song arr. MM

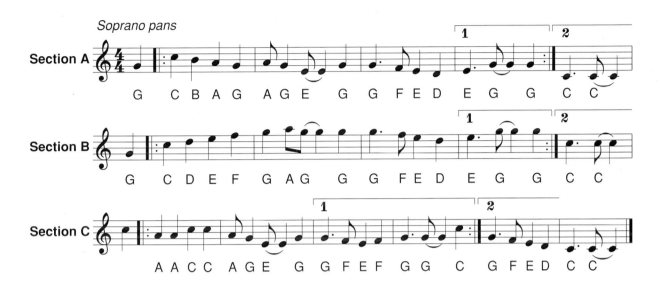

Soprano pans

Section A
G C B A G A G E G G F E D E G G C C

Section B
G C D E F G A G G G F E D E G G C C

Section C
A A C C A G E G G F E F G G C G F E D C C

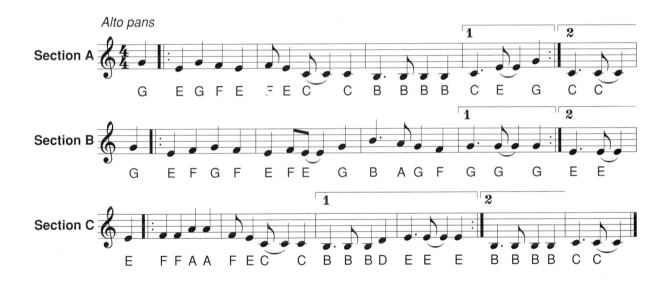

Alto pans

Section A
G E G F E F E C C B B B B C E G C C

Section B
G E F G F E F E G B A G F G G G E E

Section C
E F F A A F E C C B B B D E E E B B B B C C

Charley Marley

Jamaican folk song arr. MM

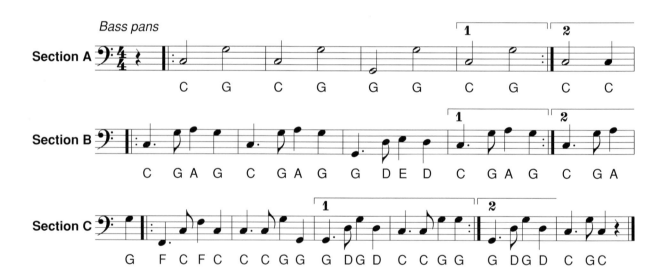

Listening to music inspired by carnivals

Listen to three excerpts of music inspired by carnivals and answer the following questions in your book. You may have to listen to each excerpt more than once.

Prelude and Variations on *Carnival of Venice* by Lalliet (track 39)

1a What is the solo instrument that plays this piece? Which instrument plays the accompaniment?

1b i How many *different* chords are used in the accompaniment? (Remember the same chord may be used a number of times – you only have to count them once each.)

ii Using the Roman numerals I, IV or V, write down the numbers of the *different* chords you counted in b(i).

iii Which of the following best describes the way in which these chords are played? (Examples of each are shown below.)

block chords

arpeggio chords

oom cha chords

broken chords

Being for the benefit of Mr Kite by John Lennon and Paul McCartney (track 40)

This Beatles' song advertises a circus performance 'for the benefit of Mr Kite'. Circus performances are often associated with carnivals and times of celebration.

2a When the words begin they are accompanied by a cymbal and other instruments. Which *two* beats of the bar does the cymbal emphasize?

i 1 and 2
ii 1 and 3
iii 1 and 4
iv 2 and 3
v 2 and 4

2b As well as the cymbal, name *one* other instrumental sound that accompanies the voice in the first verse.

2c Verse 2 ends with the words:

'and of course Henry the horse dances the waltz.'

A number of changes happen in the music *after* this line. Briefly describe *three* of these changes.

2d Is this song successful in describing the atmosphere of a circus? Describe two features of the piece that you think work really well.

Le carnaval romain (The Roman carnival) by Hector Berlioz (track 41)

3a Describe any three ways in which the composer creates a carnival atmosphere in this piece of music.

3b What changes in the music occur after the first trumpet fanfare?

3c Name two percussion instruments used in this excerpt.

Improvising melodies over chords – I, IV, V break

Share out the parts and as a class perform *I, IV, V break* printed below.

I, IV, V break

Melody

E C G E C A F C F

G E C E G D G

Chords

C F

C G

Bass

C G A G F C D C

C G A G G D E D

Notice that the melody of *I, IV, V break* is made up of chord notes. When the chord changes, new chord notes are used to extend the melody (make it longer).

Improvise a chord-note melody over the chords and bass of *I, IV, V break*.

a   using chord notes only

C E G F A C

C E G G B D

b   using chord notes and some passing notes (in-between notes)

·   C d E f G F g A bb C

C d E f G G a B c D

Voices in layers

Adding vocal layers

On the road by Patrick Allen

Sing voice 1 all together first.

Voice 1

We're mov-ing on   for - ward to - ge - ther,   we know we'll get_ there,   hea-ven knows how.

Stead-i - ly,   sure - ly,   we   know the road is rough,   hea-vy the load.

Next, sing voice 2 all together.

Voice 2

We're mov-ing on   for - ward to - ge - ther,   we know we'll get_ there,   hea-ven knows how.

Stead-i - ly,   sure - ly,   we   know the road is rough,   hea-vy the load.

Notice that:

- Voice 2 sings the same melody as Voice 1 three notes higher.
- Voice 1 begins on the note C and Voice 2 begins on the note E.
- When the two voices sing together in 3rds, a satisfying, blended harmony is created. Try it!

Finally learn Voice 3. This is an ostinato part and should be repeated throughout.

Voice 3

Doom   doom _____ ba   doom

Sing all three voices together.

Two different melodies together

African Kyrie

This piece consists of:

- Two separate call and response melodies performed one after the other. The call is sung solo, and the response is sung *tutti* (everyone).

- A section in which the two melodies are sung together.

When two separate melodies are combined in this way, the texture of the music is said to be **polyphonic**.

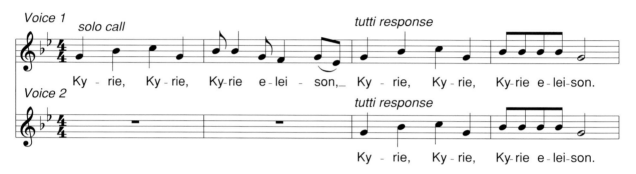

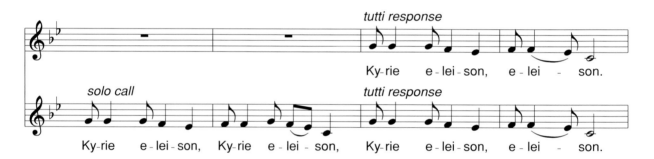

Singing chords

Journey's end **by Chris Hiscock**

More vocal layers (voice parts) can be added to a song by splitting up the notes of chords and giving them to different voice parts. Singing chord notes together creates vocal harmony.

In *Journey's end* voices 1, 2 and 3 are based on the chord sequence: C, Dm, G, C. Learn each voice part all together first, beginning with voice 1, before singing all three parts in harmony.

Voice 1

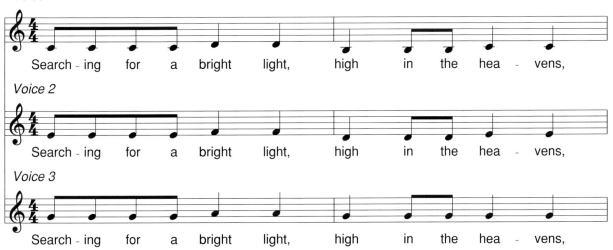

Search - ing for a bright light, high in the hea - vens,

Voice 2

Search - ing for a bright light, high in the hea - vens,

Voice 3

Search - ing for a bright light, high in the hea - vens,

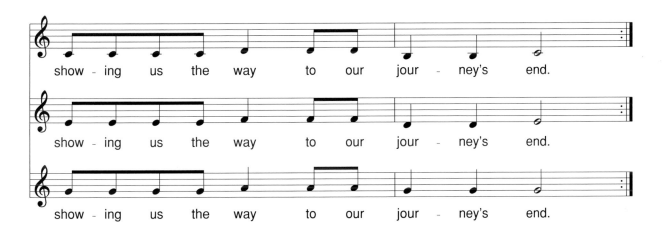

show - ing us the way to our jour - ney's end.

show - ing us the way to our jour - ney's end.

show - ing us the way to our jour - ney's end.

Finally add the descant melody as voice 4:

Voice 4 (descant)

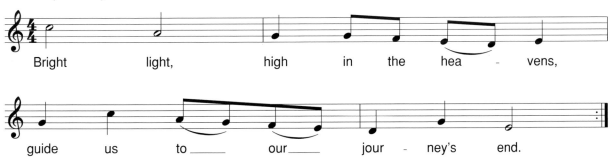

Bright light, high in the hea - vens,

guide us to _____ our _____ jour - ney's end.

Voices and vocal music

The human voice is the most versatile of all instruments. Since the beginning of humankind, throughout the world singing has been the most important, the cheapest, and the most available way of making music. Everyone can sing!

There are many different ways of singing. Solo singing, unison singing, singing in harmony, singing without instruments (called *a cappella*), singing with instruments are just some of them.

There are also many different types of occasion when people sing. They sing when they are happy and when they are sad. They sing to celebrate and they sing to encourage. They sing at work and for enjoyment.

1   Below are some examples of occasions when there might be singing. Think of a type of song associated with each:

a work	g concerts
b protests	h sports events
c for fun	i to send a baby to sleep
d rituals and worship	
e national days	j TV and radio drama
f street entertainment	k story telling

2   Look at the pictures opposite. What types of singing do they show? What types of occasion are they?

Human voices vary in pitch (some are high and some are low). This makes it possible to sing harmonies in layers using these different pitched voices.

The most important vocal layers and voice types are:

Soprano: a high woman's voice, or the highest treble (children's) voice
Alto: a low woman's voice, or a low treble voice
Tenor: the highest male voice*
Bass: the lowest male voice.

* There is a very rare male voice called a counter-tenor which is higher than a tenor, but it is seldom heard. Another male voice is a baritone which is not as deep as a bass, but can sing bass parts.

a Live rock concert

b Singers in an African village

c Opera

d Singing at a rugby match

Voices together

Tintinnabulum by Karl Jenkins

Listen to *Tintinnabulum* (track 42), a piece for female voices, strings and percussion by Karl Jenkins. *Tintinnabulum* is one of a set of pieces called *Adiemus, songs of sanctuary* ('sanctuary' means a place of safety).

When composing this piece, Karl Jenkins was inspired by musical ideas from Celtic, eastern European, African, Maori and other world musics. One feature that is common to vocal music from each of these regions is *fortissimo* (loud) singing with no *vibrato* (a slight wavering of pitch). Karl Jenkins tried to capture this style of singing in his music.

Follow the words printed in the left hand column below and opposite, and listen out for each of the vocal and backing features shown in the right hand columns. The sections are numbered for easy reference.

	words	vocal features	backing features
1	E emaka maya e emaka maya amani e amabie amani e amabi e E emaka maya e emaka maya amani e amabie amani e amabi e	two voice parts together	strings play a drone 'tremolo' string and percussion chords added
2	E emaka maya e emaka maya amani e amabi e amabi e abadi ama amaka aia a amadi adea abedia akema ya abedia akema ya akema yawe abadi abadia Abadia abadia abadi abadia badia badia	voices in unison	
3	E emaka maya e emaka maya amani e amabi e amabi e abadi ama amaka aia a amadi adea abedia akema ya abedia akemaya akema yawe abadi abadia Abadia abadia abadi abadia badia badia	voices in unison voices in harmony voices in unison voices in harmony	
4	nemus nadiemus nadiea nemus nadiemus nadiea remus radiemus radiea remus radiemus radiea	voices sing in 3rds	cymbal roll cymbal roll

5	ake manama wenama latis
	  ake manama wenama latis
	ake manama wenama latis
	  ake manama wenama latis
	ake manama wenama ratis
	  ake manama wenama ratis
	ake manama wenama yatis
	  ake manama wenama yatis
	ake manama wenama yatis
		voices echo each other	

			cymbal roll and crash

6	Ayamaya ka
	   ayamaeh
	ayamaya ka
	   ayamaeh
	ayamaya kama
	   ayamaeh
	ayamaya ka
	   ayamaeh
	ayamaya kama
	   ayamaeh
	ayamaya ka
	   ayamaeh
	ayamaya kama
	   ayamaeh
	ayamaya ka
	   ayamaeh
		voices sing a **call** in harmony and a **response** in unison	strings play a drone 'tremolo'

7	voice 1 **solo improvisations** voice 2 **ayamaeh** (repeat ad lib*) voice 3 e **amaye** (repeat ad lib) voice 4 e ———————————	response, some sing a drone on 'e'; solo vocal improvisations	strings stop, voices continue over percussion, cymbal roll to end.

* repeat as many times as you like

Adiemus could be sung by most school choirs with a little adaptation

Voices together: listening

You will hear five pieces of vocal music (tracks 43–47). Each one is different. The five pieces are:

1   *Borana dance*   Traditional

2   *Country life*   Traditional

3   *Fair Phyllis* John Farmer

4   *Deep river* Spiritual

5   *Only you*   Clarke

Listed in the three boxes below are features which might describe these pieces of music. From each box, choose *one* feature to match the music best.

Note that:

● You do not have to use each description – some may be incorrect.

● You may use any description more than once if you choose.

a

types of voice

i   female voices

ii   male voices

iii   mixed voices

iv   children's voices

v   crowd singing

b

vocal features

i   only the lead singer sings the words

ii   call and response

iii   singing in unison

iv   *a cappella*

v   voices echo and imitate each other

vi   singing in harmony

c

where this music might be heard

i   in a chapel in the southern states of America

ii   in a recording studio

iii   at an African tribal celebration

iv   on a protest march

v   in the inn after a day's work

vi   at the court of Queen Elizabeth I

Seventeenth-century madrigal singers

A gospel choir

Ragtime music

Ragtime is a style of music that grew up in the late nineteenth century in the cities of North America. It is one of several types of music that had a great influence on the early jazz of New Orleans.

A great deal of early ragtime was written for the piano. This was mainly because there was a large market for printed piano music among amateur musicians, and once the ragtime piano style caught on, many composers of ragtime pieces made a lot of money.

This type of music spread like wildfire across the whole of the USA. Piano music, ragtime songs, and ragtime dance bands became the popular music of the time.

The most important composer of ragtime was **Scott Joplin** (1868–1917) whose music inspired generations of popular and classical musicians. Joplin was one of the first black musicians to become rich and famous in the profession, and is considered to be probably the finest of all ragtime composers.

Scott Joplin playing a piano rag

Joplin's advice to pianists who wished to play ragtime was: 'Play slowly until you catch the swing, and never play ragtime fast at any time.'

The Entertainer

Scott Joplin arr. J. Moutrie and CH

Part 2a (optional)

E F F# G E F G D F E

A A G F# G A F# G A B

E F F G E F G D F E E F F

G E F G E F E G E F G E F E G E F G D F E | E C

The film *The Sting* used Joplin's *The Entertainer* in the sound track

The features of ragtime

The main features of Scott Joplin's ragtime music are:

1   Metre
A march beat in $\frac{2}{4}$ time with a steady left-hand vamp (oom-cha rhythm) based on chords which is heard throughout the piece.

cha   cha
oom   oom   *(etc.)*

Note: Joplin also wrote ragtime waltzes in $\frac{3}{4}$, but these are much less common.

2   Structure
A number of contrasting sections similar to those of the military march.

3   Melody
a   **Question and answer melodies** that contrast syncopated leaps with stepwise movement.
b   **Chromatic melodies** in which part, or parts of the melody move up or down using the smallest steps possible, i.e. semitones. A chromatic melody uses part of a **chromatic scale** (see below).

A chromatic scale ascends or descends **by semitones** from any note to the next note **with the same name**. There are twelve semitones in an octave (see below).

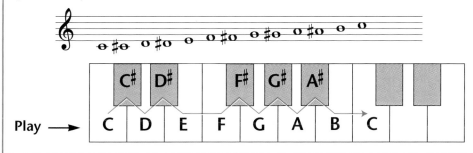

Creole jazz band from New Orleans

In pairs, one person plays the opening phrase (the first two bars) of *The Entertainer* over and over without stopping, and the second person claps an even pulse and counts aloud the main beats of the bar.

Person 1 (play)							
Person 2 (count and clap)	1	and	2	and	1	and	2	and
	clap	clap	clap	clap	clap	clap	clap	clap

c **Syncopated** melodies which have rhythms that emphasize weak beats in a bar rather than strong beats. For example, notes of syncopated melodies arrive just before the main beats of a bar, and make the music swing.

The Entertainer contains a good example of a syncopated melody.

Now you know this piece, try the exercise above to help you really come to understand syncopation.

Now try to work out what the melody of *The Entertainer* would sound like without syncopation. What would need to happen? Would the piece sound the same? What would be different?

d **Melodic passages** in parallel 3rds or 6ths. The main melody of *The Entertainer* demonstrates each of these melodic features (see below).

Note: This is the original version of Joplin's melody, not the arrangement printed on pages 57–8.

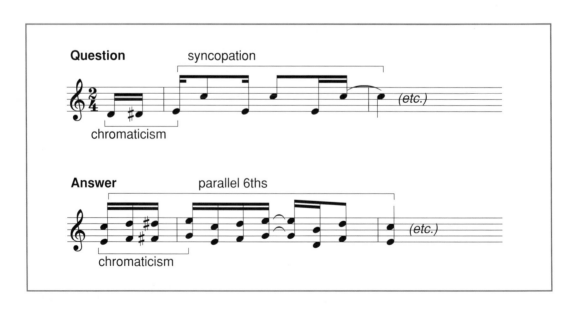

Listening to Rag-time dance

Listen to *Rag-time dance* by Scott Joplin (track 48). There are seven sections in the piece. Some sections are shorter than others. Here is the plan of the music. Follow it as you listen (don't forget to go back for the repeats).

intro ||: A :||: B :||: C :||: D :||: E :||: F :||

Near the end of the piece, Scott Joplin asks the performer to start stamping on each beat. He calls this 'stop time'. This is what is printed on the music:

Notice: to get the desired effect of 'stop time', that the pianist will please *stamp* the heel of one foot heavily upon the floor at the word 'stamp'. Do not raise the toe from the floor while stamping.

Why you think Joplin asks for this effect?

Syncopation rapidly spread to dance music. The charleston became popular in the 1920s.

Now listen to each section (intro, A, B, C, D, E, F) of *Rag-time dance* played separately in order, without its repeat.

Match each section with one of the statements below and write the answers in your books:

1 This section begins with a foot stamp and the melody is broken up.

2 This is the shortest section and is played without chords. The melody ascends (goes up) and descends (goes down) with many chromatic notes.

3 In this section a question/answer melody is repeated three times with some small changes in each repeat. The 'question' begins by moving in steps whilst the answer has more leaps and syncopations.

4 This section contains a complete descending chromatic scale, repeated twice.

5 This section has a higher pitched melody beginning with a 'short–short–long' rhythm, and the following melodic shape:

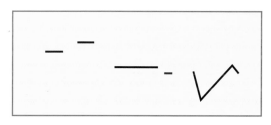

6 This section is lower in pitch than all the others and has a melody that repeats twice. The backing pattern begins: oom-cha, oom-cha, oom-cha-cha.

7 This section begins with repeated, instead of leaping, oom-cha backing chords. There is a silence with two stamps before the last two notes.

Vamping the chords

You have already learned about chords and riff patterns earlier in this book (see Project 4, pages 38–9). To perform ragtime backings, chords are played in a repeating oom-cha pattern called a **vamp**. A vamp is usually played by the left hand on a piano or keyboard, and is used in many types of music as well as ragtime.

Learning to vamp is an important keyboard skill, and is well worth practising. Vamp patterns are best learned using *both* hands, dividing the notes between them. Later you may learn to play vamps with your left hand alone.

Below are a number of march vamp patterns based on the chord of C. They become more and more difficult! Attempt as many patterns as you can.

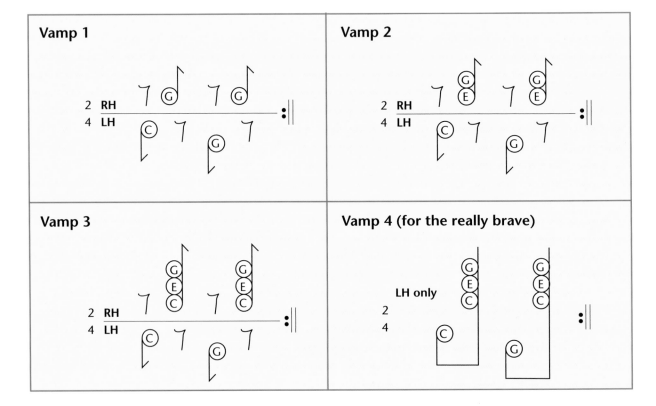

Next try the same vamp patterns but this time use the chord of F and then the chord of G.

Vamping a waltz

A waltz always has an oom-cha-cha pattern. Here is Vamp 1 in this pattern:

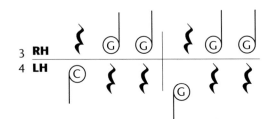

Work out for yourself Vamps 2, 3 and 4 in a waltz oom-cha-cha pattern.

Vamping a chord sequence

Finally, using one of the vamp patterns with which you feel comfortable, vamp the whole of the following chord sequences:

March
C / / / C / / / F / / / F / / / C / / / C / / / G / / / G / / /

Waltz
C / / C / / F / / F / / C / / C / / G / / G / /

Syncopations

Listen to four excerpts of music and answer the following questions:

Sikuriadas (track 49)

Pan pipe music from South America.

1a There are 4 beats in a bar.
Bar 1 has 4 steady beats to set the tempo. In which bar do you *first* hear syncopation?

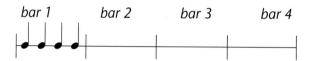

1b Which instrument plays the *melody* after the pan pipes stop? Choose from:

  i   mandolin

  ii   guitar

  iii violin

  iv harp

1c i   What happens to the tempo after the pan pipes stop playing the melody?

    ii   What effect does this have on the music?

Deep Henderson (track 50)

Traditional jazz performed by King Oliver and his Dixie Syncopators.

2a After a short introduction the tenor saxophone plays the first solo.

  i   Which instrument plays the second solo?

  ii   Which instrument plays the third solo?

2b Which instrument in this piece never plays syncopated but keeps a steady beat? Choose from :

  i   piano

  ii   clarinet

  iii trumpet

  iv tuba

  v   saxophone

2c What difference does the syncopation make to this type of music?

Golliwogg's cakewalk by Claude Debussy (track 51)

3a There are two beats in a bar in this piece. In which bar number do you *first* hear syncopation?

3b Name one or more ways in which the introduction to this piece is like the introduction to *The Entertainer*.

3c *Golliwogg's cakewalk* was composed soon after ragtime music became popular in France. Name three features of this piece which tell us that the composer was inspired by ragtime music.

Principia by Steve Martland (track 52)

4a Does this piece have:

  i   2 beats in a bar

  ii   3 beats in a bar

  iii a metre which keeps changing?

4b Which section of the orchestra is *not* included in this piece:

  i   strings

  ii   woodwind

  iii brass

  iv percussion?

4c This piece is full of little stops. What effect does this have on the music?

When I'm sixty-four

by John Lennon and Paul McCartney

1 When I get ol - der los - ing my hair _ man - y years from now,
2 I could be han - dy mend - ing a fuse when your lights have gone,
3 Send me a post - card drop me a line stat - ing point of view,

Will you still be send - ing me a va - len - tine, _ birth - day greet - ing,
You can knit a swea - ter by the fi - re - side, _ Sun - day morn - ings,
In - di - cate pre - cise - ly what you mean to say, _ yours sin - cere - ly,

bot - tle of wine? If I'd been out 'till quar - ter to three would you lock the
go for a ride. Do - ing the gar - den dig - ging the weeds who could ask for
want - ing a - way. Give me your ans - wer, fill in a form, mine for - e - ver -

Fine last verse

door? Will you still need me, will you still feed me _ when I'm six - ty - four?
more? Will you still need me, will you still feed me _ when I'm six - ty - four?
more. Will you still need me, will you still feed me _ when I'm six - ty - four?

1 *Tacet (voices silent)*
2 Ev - 'ry sum - mer we can rent a cot - tage on the Isle of Wight, if it's not too

You'll be ol - der too, _____ And if you
dear. We shall scrimp and save, _____ Grand - chil - dren

DC

say the word, __ I could stay with you. _____
on your knee, __ Ve - ra, Chuck and Dave. _____